NATIONAL COMMISSION FOR MEN

SILENT SCARS

REAL STORIES OF CRIMES AGAINST MEN IN INDIA

DR. NITYA PRAKASH

"Author at his best"
-Hindustan Times

ink Scribe

National Commission for Men

Publisher: Inkscribe Media Pvt. Ltd

ISBN Number: 978-1-966421-49-8

To Maa
Your strength shaped my soul,
your silence taught me resilience.
This book is a tribute to everything you endured,
and everything you

Acknowledgement

Writing *National Commission for Men: Silent Scars – Real Stories of Crimes Against Men in India* has been a journey through unspoken truths and often uncomfortable realities. This book is more than a narrative—it is a **plea for recognition**, a **demand for justice**, and a **call to conscience** in a country where male suffering is often dismissed, ignored, or ridiculed.

Many of the stories you will read in these pages are drawn from **real-life incidents**, documented in courts and reported in the media. But some—perhaps the most painful—are rooted in **my own personal experiences** or those of people very close to me. I have seen firsthand how societal denial, legal prejudice, and emotional neglect can erode even the strongest of men.

To the survivors who found the courage to speak, even when the world called them weak—you are heroes in the truest sense. To the families who continue to fight for justice, even after losing loved ones to false cases, mental trauma, or societal pressure—this book is for you.

To the lawyers, NGOs, and men's rights activists who stand up for fairness, often without applause or funding—you give strength to this movement.

A very special thanks to those who challenged me to write this book, even when the topic was considered controversial. Your encouragement reminded me why this needed to be told.

And let me say this with unwavering clarity:

This book is not anti-women.

It is not an attack on feminism, nor a denial of the struggles women have faced throughout history. **In fact, we need the National Commission for Women now more than ever.** But at the same time, in the world's largest democracy, **we also need a National Commission for Men.**

Because protecting women should not come at the cost of **neglecting men**.

Because equality is not about taking sides—it's about **listening to every voice, especially the unheard**.

If we fail to act now, then someday, in a book like this, the next chapter could be about **someone you know**—your son, your friend, your brother, your colleague.

It's time we stop waiting.

It's time we start listening.

It's time we rise—**for our men, too.**

— *Dr. Nitya Prakash*

Entrepreneur, Author & Crusader for Balanced Justice

Contents

- ➢ Faced false cheating and molestation charges when he tried to exit.
- ➢ Surveillance footage helped him get bail.

- ➢ Interviews with NGOs like *Save Indian Family Foundation* and *Men Welfare Trust*.
- ➢ Role of legal experts pushing for gender-neutral laws.
- ➢ Suggestions for reforms in laws like IPC 498A, POSH, and rape laws.

- ➢ Social taboos around male vulnerability.
- ➢ Role of media, schools, and families in addressing male abuse.
- ➢ Call to action for balanced gender discourse.

- ➢ A Bengaluru-based software engineer who died by suicide in December 2024, leaving behind a 24-page note and an 81-minute video.
- ➢ Alleged harassment by his estranged wife and family.
- ➢ Sparked national debate on misuse of dowry laws and need for gender-neutral legislation.

- ➢ March 2025: Muskan Rastogi and her lover Sahil Shukla allegedly murdered her husband and concealed his dismembered body in a cement drum.
- ➢ Case exposed brutality of domestic abuse against men.

Chapter 1

The Invisible Victims

India's struggle for gender justice has been one of the most important social revolutions of our time. From dismantling patriarchal norms to amplifying the voices of women who were denied autonomy, dignity, and protection for centuries, we have witnessed profound progress in building a more equal society. Laws have been passed, rights have been reclaimed, and voices have been rightfully raised. And yet, amid this essential journey—one that must and should continue—there exists a **blind spot**, one so deep that most refuse to even acknowledge it.

That blind spot is **male victimhood**.

This book begins with a hard truth: **men, too, can be victims.** They can be broken, manipulated, abused, falsely accused, silenced, or even driven to death. But because society has built a myth of male invulnerability, their pain often goes unnoticed—and worse, it is ridiculed.

From a young age, boys are taught not to cry, not to feel, not to speak of pain. Strength is defined by suppression. Vulnerability is labeled weakness. And asking for help? That's seen as a betrayal of their masculinity. As a result, **men who suffer—emotionally, physically, or legally—do so in the shadows.**

And those shadows are darker than we care to admit.

The Numbers That No One Wants to Talk About

In 2022, over **72,000 married men in India died by suicide**. Most of them cited domestic issues, emotional pressure, legal harassment, or relationship breakdowns as the trigger. In contrast, **27,000 married women** took their lives in the same year—a grave number, yes, but one that receives far more attention, support, and institutional sympathy. Why is the death of 72,000 married men treated as an afterthought?

These are not isolated cases. They are the **outcome of a systemic failure**—where men have no support structures, no legal recourse in many cases, and no national platform to voice their trauma.

When the Law Is a Sword, Not a Shield

One of the most controversial and debated sections of the Indian Penal Code is **Section 498A**, originally designed to protect women from dowry-related abuse. It was created with noble intent—to shield women from torture, blackmail, and violence in their marital homes. And in many cases, it has saved lives. But over time, this section has also become **a tool of legal vengeance**.

Even the **Supreme Court of India**, in its 2014 landmark judgment in *Arnesh Kumar vs. State of Bihar*, noted the misuse of 498A, cautioning law enforcement agencies against making automatic arrests. The judgment stated clearly that **entire families—elderly parents, sisters, and even distant relatives—have been arrested without preliminary inquiry**, often based on unverified complaints. The impact? Reputations destroyed. Careers lost. Families torn apart. Innocent lives derailed.

And yet, there is no equivalent legal protection for men. No provision that criminalizes **false accusations** with the same urgency. No relief mechanism for a man who is emotionally manipulated or physically abused by his spouse. While **women have access to the Domestic Violence Act, there is no law in India that recognizes domestic violence against men.**

The Stigma of Speaking Up

Even when men try to raise their voices, they are often silenced by mockery or disbelief:

> **Police officials laugh them off**, telling them to "man up."

> **Friends abandon them**, branding them as weak or emasculated.

> **Families pressure them to stay silent**, fearing societal shame.

> **Courts demand mountains of proof**, often overlooking male emotional trauma.

In short, the very system that should provide justice **fails to even acknowledge their pain.**

This silence isn't just societal—it is systemic. There are **no government-run shelters** for abused men. **No national helpline** exclusively for male victims. **No commission**, no dedicated ministry, and no comprehensive study funded by the state to understand this emerging crisis. And yet, **every year, tens of thousands of men silently suffer, and many don't survive**.

This Book Is Not a Counter-Narrative to Women's Rights

Let us be very clear: **this book does not deny the suffering of women**. It does not seek to dilute the importance of the women's movement. If anything, we support and celebrate the hard-won gains of women across India. But true gender equality means fairness for all—not privilege for one at the cost of another.

This book is **not anti-women—it is pro-justice.** It calls for a legal and social system that **sees victims, regardless of gender**, and offers protection, compassion, and due process to all.

What Lies Ahead

In the chapters that follow, you will meet men who were:

> ➤ Falsely accused and arrested,

> ➤ Emotionally and physically abused by their spouses,

> ➤ Denied custody of their children,

> ➤ Manipulated through the legal system,

> ➤ Publicly humiliated and socially boycotted,

> ➤ And in some heartbreaking cases—driven to take their own lives.

These are not nameless figures. They are **engineers, bankers, teachers, fathers, brothers, sons, and husbands**. Their stories are real. Their pain is undeniable. Their fight for justice is ongoing.

By sharing these stories, we do not seek to ignite a war between genders. We seek to illuminate a **blind spot in India's justice system**—and make a heartfelt case for the creation of a **National Commission for Men**.

Because silence is not strength. And ignoring suffering—no matter who endures it—is not justice.

Let this book be the beginning of a long-overdue conversation.

Let it be a mirror to a society that has for too long seen only one side of the story.

Let it be a voice for the invisible victims.

Chapter 2

The Engineer Who Never Returned

Satish Kumar, a 29-year-old software engineer in Bangalore, was known among his colleagues as a quiet, hardworking professional. An introvert by nature, Satish preferred coding over coffee breaks, and his dedication at the IT firm where he worked earned him steady promotions and the admiration of his peers.

In January 2019, Satish's body was found hanging from a ceiling fan in his rented apartment. What initially seemed like a tragic suicide quickly unraveled into a devastating case of alleged false accusation and social persecution.

The Beginning of the End

Satish had been in a relationship with a woman he met through a matrimonial website. It was short-lived—by his account, she was controlling, emotionally manipulative, and verbally abusive. After a few months of disagreements, he broke it off.

What followed was a nightmare.

Two months after their breakup, the woman filed a **First Information Report (FIR)** under **Section 376 (rape)** and **Section 417 (cheating)** of the Indian Penal Code. She claimed Satish had established a physical relationship with her on the pretext of marriage—a claim that, under Indian law, could attract imprisonment up to life.

Satish was arrested and spent 17 days in judicial custody before being released on bail. Though he maintained his innocence, the damage was done. His company suspended him pending inquiry. His landlord asked him to vacate the premises. Friends distanced themselves, and his own relatives were hesitant to speak in his defense, fearing societal backlash.

The Suicide Note

When Satish died, he left behind a detailed suicide note. In it, he wrote:

"I did not rape anyone. I loved her truly. When I realized we were not compatible, I stepped away respectfully. I never lied about marriage. But she turned my honesty into a weapon. The police treated me like a criminal. My friends think I'm guilty. My job is gone. My life is gone. I can't live this way anymore."

It was a heartbreaking testament to how a single accusation— without trial or conviction—can destroy a life.

Post-Mortem Justice

After his death, media outlets picked up the story. A local news channel ran a primetime segment titled *"When Law Is Abused: The Other Side of #MeToo."* An NGO called **Men's Rights Association** held a candlelight vigil in his memory, demanding the government institute gender-neutral laws on sexual assault.

The girl, under public pressure, withdrew her complaint weeks later. She said she had acted out of "emotional anger" and "felt betrayed."

No legal action was taken against her for the false complaint.

Satish's parents filed a civil suit in court, seeking action against her for abetment of suicide. The case is still pending.

The Larger Conversation

Satish's story is not an isolated one. Across India, cases of alleged false accusations of rape or molestation, especially under the clause of **"promise to marry"**, have steadily risen. A 2020 Delhi Commission of Women (DCW) report found that **over 53%** of rape cases in the city that year were filed by women in live-in relationships where the promise of marriage fell through.

This raises difficult but important questions:

- ➢ Should broken relationships always be treated as criminal betrayal?
- ➢ Should police arrests happen without preliminary investigations?
- ➢ What about the presumption of innocence?
- ➢ Satish did not live to see these questions answered.

But his story endures, echoing the silent suffering of thousands of Indian men who are presumed guilty simply because they are men.

He was an engineer, a son, a dreamer—and above all, a human being whose truth went unheard.

Until now.

Chapter 3

The Banker and the Dowry Trap

Vikram Singh, a 33-year-old assistant manager at a reputed public sector bank in Delhi, was the pride of his family. Hailing from a modest background in Haryana, he had worked his way up through diligence and discipline. A secure job, an own flat in Dwarka, and a government health card—Vikram had all the markers of a "good match" in India's matrimonial market.

In 2021, he got married through an arranged setup. The wedding was grand, by middle-class standards—nearly 700 guests, multiple rituals, and a dowry that Vikram's family claims was "voluntarily given" by the bride's side. But within months, cracks began to appear.

A Marriage Turned Minefield

Vikram's wife, Priya, had difficulty adjusting to his joint family. She refused to do household chores, insisted on frequent expensive outings, and picked fights with his parents. When Vikram tried to mediate, he became the target.

Tensions escalated when Priya left the house after just eight months of marriage, citing harassment by Vikram and his family. A few weeks later, he was served with legal notices under:

- ➤ **Section 498A IPC** (Cruelty to wife by husband and relatives),

- ➤ **Section 406** (criminal breach of trust for dowry),

- ➤ **Section 34** (common intent), and a **Maintenance Application under Section 125 CrPC**.

Within days, police arrived at Vikram's flat and arrested him along with his aged mother and younger unmarried sister. His father, a retired school teacher, collapsed from the shock and was hospitalized.

The Fallout

Vikram spent nine days in Tihar Jail before securing bail. His suspension from the bank followed, pending departmental enquiry. Friends and relatives kept their distance. His fiancée's side had claimed he was abusive, and in a society where perception is often more powerful than truth, the label of "wife-beater" stuck like glue.

When Priya was asked by the court to present medical records, police complaints filed during the time she stayed at her in-laws, or any corroborating witness, **she failed to provide any concrete evidence**.

After two years of litigation, the court finally **dismissed the criminal case**, citing *lack of evidence* and *malicious intent to harass*. Vikram was acquitted, but by then:

➢ His mother's health had deteriorated severely due to mental trauma.

➢ His sister, once a topper in DU, was denied multiple jobs after police verification records flagged her arrest.

➢ Vikram returned to his bank, but the transfer, stigma, and emotional burnout had left him a shell of the man he once was.

The Cost of Misuse

Vikram now volunteers with a men's rights NGO, speaking at events and legal literacy camps. "I don't deny that women suffer," he says, "but the law should not become a weapon in the hands of those who want to settle personal scores."

The Supreme Court has, time and again, commented on the misuse of Section 498A. In one of its rulings, it stated:

"It is a matter of serious concern that large numbers of cases continue to be filed under Section 498A alleging harassment of married women... without any check or verification. Many such complaints are not bona fide."

Despite this, **there is no legal penalty for filing a false dowry case**, unless the accused goes through the difficult process of proving malicious prosecution.

The Stigma Remains

Even after being acquitted, Vikram finds it hard to date again. "Every girl Googles you. Every family does a background check. Even if you're cleared, you're never clean," he says.

What began as a matrimonial alliance ended in a life-altering legal war. For Vikram, and thousands of Indian men like him, **the damage is not just legal—it's social, psychological, and permanent.**

Chapter 4

Child Custody, But Not for Him

Rajeev Malhotra looked every bit the devoted father—he attended PTA meetings, helped his daughter with math homework, and never missed a birthday. A mid-level executive in a Mumbai-based logistics company, Rajeev had built his life around his daughter Rhea, who was just seven years old when his world collapsed.

What started as a failing marriage ended in a bitter custody battle—one where Rajeev found himself fighting not only his estranged wife but also a judicial and societal system that simply didn't believe **fathers could be primary caregivers**.

The Breakdown

Rajeev and Shalini married in 2011. Their relationship had been arranged through community networks, and for the first few years, they managed to maintain the façade of a stable home. But behind closed doors, Shalini frequently engaged in psychological abuse—shouting, belittling, and sometimes turning violent during arguments.

In 2017, after repeated attempts at reconciliation, Rajeev moved out and filed for divorce, citing mental cruelty. Shalini retaliated swiftly, filing for maintenance under Section 125 CrPC and seeking **exclusive custody of their daughter**, alleging that Rajeev was "aggressive" and "unfit to be a father."

The courts, as per standard practice, **granted interim custody to the mother**. Rajeev was allowed two Sundays a month for supervised visitation at a neutral location. Rhea would cry at the end of each meeting, clinging to her father, but Rajeev could do little except promise to fight harder.

The Legal Labyrinth

Rajeev's legal team gathered witness statements from neighbors who had heard loud fights—almost always initiated by Shalini. A therapist who had counseled the couple also supported Rajeev's claim of being emotionally abused. But it didn't matter.

"Indian courts operate under the **tacit presumption that a mother is the default caregiver**," Rajeev says. "Even if the father is more capable, more available, or more affectionate—it rarely counts."

Despite no evidence of abuse or neglect, the Family Court ruled in favor of Shalini, granting her permanent custody. Rajeev was allowed four days a month, still under supervision, and barred from overnight stays. His request to take Rhea on a short vacation was denied twice.

He appealed in the High Court—but the process dragged on for four years.

The Emotional Cost

During these years, Rajeev saw Rhea become more withdrawn. Her school grades dropped. On one occasion, her teacher privately told Rajeev that Rhea had mentioned "wanting to live with papa." But Rajeev had no legal standing to act on it.

The final blow came in 2022 when Rajeev was informed that Shalini was planning to move to Australia with Rhea under a work visa. By the time his petition to block the relocation reached the Family Court, **mother and child had already flown out**.

To this day, Rajeev has not physically met Rhea again. He's allowed monthly video calls, heavily monitored, during which Rhea—now coached—barely speaks.

Fathers in Indian Courts: A Systemic Bias

Rajeev's case is far from rare. Indian family courts have an overwhelming tendency to grant custody to mothers, even when fathers are proven to be more stable or emotionally available.

Unlike countries like the UK or Australia—where **shared parenting** is legally encouraged—India lacks any legislative mandate for equal parental rights post-divorce.

The **Law Commission of India**, in its 257th report, recommended joint custody and shared parenting models. But legislative action has been sluggish, and outdated perceptions continue to dominate judicial thinking.

The Man Behind the Movement

Rajeev has since become a vocal advocate for father's rights in India. He speaks at legal panels, contributes to petitions calling for reforms in the **Guardians and Wards Act**, and runs a Telegram channel where alienated fathers share their grief and strategies.

"I'm not asking to win against Shalini," Rajeev says. "I'm asking for my daughter to have a father in her life."

The Bigger Picture

In a world where the conversation around parenting post-divorce is rapidly evolving, India remains stuck in the past—where **a mother is always good, a father is always second best**, and the child's welfare is a secondary concern.

Rajeev Malhotra is just one man. But behind him are lakhs of fathers—**bereft, forgotten, and stripped of the right to love their children freely**.

Chapter 5

Bruised Behind Closed Doors

Ankit Rawat never imagined that the worst bruises he would carry would not come from the outside world, but from the woman he had once promised to love forever.

A 34-year-old marketing professional in Chandigarh, Ankit was known among friends as soft-spoken and polite—perhaps even overly accommodating. Tall, lanky, and always smiling, he had what most would call a stable life: a decent job, a recently purchased 2BHK apartment in Zirakpur, and a marriage that, at least on paper, seemed picture-perfect.

But behind the closed doors of his home, Ankit was living a quiet nightmare—**as a victim of domestic violence.**

The Illusion of a Normal Marriage

Ankit married Rhea (name changed) in 2020 through a matrimonial website. She was independent, well-educated, and working with a multinational firm in Mohali. Their profiles matched, and so did their ambitions—or so it appeared.

Initially, the relationship was warm, filled with romantic dinners, shared vacations, and long chats about career plans. But within a year of marriage, things changed.

Rhea's behavior grew erratic. Small disagreements turned into **violent outbursts**. She would throw utensils, slap him during arguments, and once even hurled his phone at his head during a disagreement about finances. On another occasion, Ankit was forced to lock himself in the bathroom for hours to avoid her rage.

He bore it silently, believing it was a phase. Like most Indian men, he had grown up being told that "a man should never raise his voice at a woman" or "ghar ki baat ghar mein rehni chahiye." So he endured, hoping love would win.

But love doesn't leave bruises.

The Night That Changed Everything

In March 2022, a particularly violent incident escalated beyond anything Ankit had endured before.

Rhea accused him of being "emotionally unavailable" and cheating—without a shred of proof. In a fit of rage, she grabbed a metal lamp and struck him on the shoulder. He collapsed, shocked and bleeding. When he tried to reach for his phone, she slapped it away and locked herself in the bedroom.

That night, Ankit made a decision he never thought he would: he dialed **100** and called the police.

When the officers arrived, Rhea claimed that Ankit had assaulted *her*. She even showed self-inflicted scratch marks on her arm. The police laughed off Ankit's bruises and told him, *"Sir, aap jaisa aadmi ghar mein pit raha hai? Shame on you. Be a man."*

Friends Who Laughed, Not Listened

Worse than the police response was the reaction from his own circle.

When Ankit confided in close friends, they chuckled. One said, "Yaar tu toh lucky hai, biwi tere par haath daalti hai. Role reversal!" Another dismissed it with, "Bas acting mat kar. Sab adjustment hota hai shaadi mein."

Even his parents were reluctant to intervene. "Don't make a scene," his mother said. "Log kya kahenge? Divorce lene wale logon ki toh izzat hi chali jaati hai."

The **emotional isolation** was complete.

The Road to Justice—Slow, Harsh, and Unbelievable

Determined to document the abuse, Ankit began recording arguments and taking photos of injuries. He visited a local hospital, where a doctor noted "blunt force trauma to the shoulder and upper arm." Armed with evidence, he approached a lawyer.

The legal process was painfully slow. His complaint under IPC Sections **323** (voluntarily causing hurt) and **506** (criminal intimidation) was met with skepticism. The magistrate initially dismissed the plea, suggesting "mediation" would be better. It took three months, media attention, and the intervention of a men's rights NGO for the case to even be registered.

Meanwhile, Rhea filed a counter-case under **Section 498A** and **Domestic Violence Act**, accusing Ankit and his parents of mental and physical torture—turning the tables entirely.

The result? Both parties are now entangled in a **mutual legal battle**, and Ankit is back at his parents' home, fighting to clear his name while trying to heal wounds deeper than skin.

The Unseen Side of Domestic Violence

According to the National Family Health Survey (NFHS-5), around **4.4% of men in India** report having experienced physical violence at the hands of their spouses—though experts say the real number is likely much higher due to **underreporting and stigma**.

There is **no provision in Indian law that explicitly recognizes male victims of domestic violence.** The Protection of Women from Domestic Violence Act, 2005 is, by design, one-sided. Men have no recourse under this Act—even if they're being physically, emotionally, or financially abused.

Ankit's New Purpose

Today, Ankit speaks openly about his experience. He has joined a support group run by *Men Welfare Trust* and appears on webinars to talk about male trauma, legal loopholes, and social apathy.

"I'm not ashamed anymore," he says. "I was abused. I was broken. But I've rebuilt myself. If one man finds the courage to speak out after reading my story, I'll know this pain wasn't for nothing."

Behind Closed Doors, Many More Cry for Help

Ankit's story is not just a cautionary tale—it's a **mirror**. A reflection of the thousands of Indian men trapped in violent relationships, afraid of being mocked, ignored, or disbelieved. For these men, the bruises may fade, but the silence stays.

This chapter is for them.

It's time to open the door.

Chapter 6
The MeToo Misfire

Karthik Iyer, a 39-year-old associate professor at a prestigious liberal arts university in Chennai, loved teaching. A gold medallist from Jawaharlal Nehru University, his passion for gender studies and critical theory made him a favorite among students. Ironically, it was this very subject—and the movement he once supported—that nearly destroyed his life.

In October 2018, during the peak of the #MeToo movement in India, Karthik was anonymously accused of sexual misconduct on a now-deleted Twitter thread. The post did not name him directly but included enough identifying details—department, designation, publications—that it became apparent who the "predator professor" was.

The backlash was instant.

He was asked to go on immediate administrative leave. Social media mobs called for his arrest. News channels ran segments titled *"Another #MeToo Moment in Academia."* Colleagues stopped talking to him. Students began avoiding his lectures. His name, once attached to academic brilliance, was now equated with assault.

The Invisible Trial

Karthik was never served a legal notice, never summoned to court. There was no FIR. No formal complaint had ever been filed. The university's Internal Complaints Committee (ICC) launched an inquiry but faced a dilemma: without a named accuser, they had no jurisdiction.

Still, to "protect the institution's reputation," Karthik was asked to step down from his teaching responsibilities until the matter could be "resolved."

He spent the next six months in personal and professional exile. His mental health plummeted. He was prescribed anti-anxiety medication. The isolation was unbearable.

Then, a twist.

In May 2019, the anonymous user who had posted the original accusation posted a retraction, stating:

"I made a mistake. I confused identities. It was not Professor Karthik Iyer. I deeply regret the trauma caused."

But it was too late.

The Stain That Won't Wash Off

Despite the public apology, Karthik was not reinstated. The university distanced itself further, offering him a quiet resignation package. Publishers withdrew upcoming book deals. A TEDx talk he was scheduled to deliver on gender justice was canceled.

He tried to fight back. Filed a defamation suit. The case is still pending.

In interviews, Karthik later said, "I support women's voices. But justice must involve process. When it becomes a trial by hashtags, innocent people get crucified."

His story is not unique.

In the wake of the #MeToo movement, while many genuine stories emerged and much-needed conversations began, a small but significant number of **false, misdirected, or unverifiable claims** caused collateral damage—especially when amplified by social media.

Due Process vs. Digital Mob

India's judicial framework is built on the idea of *innocent until proven guilty.* But on the internet, the reverse often holds true. The mere mention of an accusation can ruin a career.

Karthik's case is a chilling reminder that **false allegations don't just harm the accused—they undermine the credibility of genuine survivors**.

According to a 2020 report by the Delhi Commission for Women (DCW), over 50% of rape cases filed in the capital were found to be fabricated or had major inconsistencies during investigation. Yet, public narratives rarely distinguish the false from the factual.

Moving Forward

Karthik now lives in Coimbatore with his parents. He writes occasionally under a pseudonym and tutors a few students online. His faith in justice remains shaky, but he hopes his story will serve as a cautionary tale—not against believing survivors, but against abandoning due process.

"Injustice to one is injustice to all," he says. "Even in movements born of truth, we must protect the truth for everyone."

His chapter is a sobering testament to the cost of a misfire.

And a reminder that justice must have two ears, not just one voice.

Chapter 7

Jailed Without Justice

Tariq Hussain was the first in his family to finish college. A soft-spoken 27-year-old from Lucknow, he worked as a junior project coordinator at a construction firm, quietly climbing the ladder of middle-class aspirations. He had dreams—saving for his sister's wedding, buying a bike, perhaps even applying for a job abroad. But those dreams came crashing down with a knock on the door that changed everything.

On a summer morning in May 2023, Tariq was arrested at his workplace. The charge? **Sexual assault** under Section 354 of the Indian Penal Code—*assault or criminal force to a woman with intent to outrage her modesty*. He was handcuffed, paraded in front of his colleagues, and taken to the local police station without any prior notice or investigation.

The Accusation

The complaint had been filed by a newly recruited intern at the same firm, who alleged that Tariq had touched her inappropriately while showing her the construction site. There were no witnesses. No medical report. No CCTV footage submitted along with the FIR. Yet, based on her statement alone, the police moved swiftly to arrest Tariq.

He was thrown into a congested lock-up, interrogated without legal counsel, and booked under **non-bailable sections**. His bail application was rejected twice. He spent the next **eight months in prison.**

Inside the Walls

Jail is no place for an innocent man. Tariq was beaten by fellow inmates who believed he was a "molester." The guards didn't intervene. He was denied proper food, his calls to family were monitored, and he missed his younger sister's wedding—a moment he had long promised her he would be there for.

His mother fell ill. His father, a retired electrician, spent their entire savings on legal fees. Meanwhile, the real evidence—the truth—was quietly waiting in a hard drive.

The Truth Uncovered

After several months, Tariq's lawyer managed to obtain surveillance footage from the construction site's security system. The footage **clearly showed Tariq maintaining professional distance** from the intern throughout the tour. At no point was there any physical contact, let alone anything remotely inappropriate.

When this footage was finally submitted in court during a bail hearing, the case began to unravel. The intern, when cross-examined, admitted that she had filed the complaint in "anger" after Tariq allegedly gave negative feedback on her work to the HR department.

The court, appalled at the misuse of the law, granted Tariq bail and eventually dismissed the case citing *lack of evidence and apparent malicious intent.*

But the damage was done.

Life After Release

Tariq returned home a broken man. His job was gone. His name was tainted. Neighbors whispered. Old friends avoided him. His mother's health had worsened. And the family now lived in debt.

What stung most was not the months he spent in prison—it was the **lack of apology**, the **lack of accountability** from those who had wronged him.

The woman who had filed the false complaint walked away without penalty. No perjury charges. No compensation. Nothing.

Justice for Whom?

Tariq's story is not an exception—it's a reflection of a systemic problem. While the need to protect women from genuine sexual harassment is paramount, the **lack of safeguards against false accusations** has led to an alarming number of wrongful arrests.

In 2022 alone, over **25% of rape cases filed in India were found to be false or fabricated during investigation** (NCRB data). Yet, the criminal justice system has no fast-track remedy for those who suffer because of these falsehoods.

There is **no statutory protection or rehabilitation** for men like Tariq. No financial aid. No state-sponsored apology. And certainly, no societal redemption.

Tariq Today

Now 28, Tariq volunteers with a legal aid NGO that helps men navigate the aftermath of false accusations. He gives talks in universities, raises awareness on gender-biased legal procedures, and advocates for a **gender-neutral approach to justice**.

He doesn't speak with anger, but with quiet resilience.

"I lost eight months of my life. I lost my job. But I didn't lose my dignity. The truth saved me. And now, I'll fight for others like me."

Tariq Hussain was jailed without justice.

But through his courage, the injustice has found a voice.

And this chapter—this truth—is his redemption.

Chapter 8

The Forgotten Elder

Shambhu Nath, 70, once lived a quiet, respected life in the old city lanes of Varanasi. A retired postmaster, he had spent over three decades in government service, never missed a day of work, and was known in his neighborhood for his uprightness and wisdom.

After retirement, he lived with his son, daughter-in-law, and two grandchildren in a modest ancestral home. He had always imagined his twilight years would be peaceful—filled with temple visits, evening chats, and watching his grandchildren grow.

But in 2020, his life took a cruel, undignified turn—one that would see him **falsely accused, thrown out of his own home, and left to sleep on a park bench**.

When Love Turns Legal

The trouble began subtly.

Shambhu's daughter-in-law, Meenakshi, began arguing frequently—over meals, household chores, and money. She demanded that the house be transferred to her name. When Shambhu refused, saying it would eventually go to his son anyway, she became hostile.

What followed was shocking: Meenakshi filed a complaint under **Section 12 of the Domestic Violence Act**, claiming that her father-in-law was mentally harassing her, creating a toxic living environment, and threatening her safety. She alleged that Shambhu constantly fought with her, restricted her movements, and even tried to evict her from the house.

With just her verbal statement and no evidence, the court **granted her interim protection**—effectively restricting Shambhu from entering or interfering in the shared household.

The result? The man who had built the house brick by brick was legally **barred from entering his own home.**

Abandoned Overnight

Shambhu tried to reason with his son, pleading for a resolution. But his son, torn between duty and domestic harmony, remained silent. One evening, while returning from a temple visit, Shambhu found the locks changed and his belongings dumped in a garbage bag on the porch.

He knocked. No one opened the door.

With nowhere to go, he wandered for hours before settling on a park bench near Assi Ghat. That night, he slept under the open sky, clutching a tattered shawl.

The System That Failed Him

Over the next few weeks, Shambhu approached the local police and magistrate's office to present his side. He had ownership papers. He had no criminal record. He had neighbors willing to testify to his character.

But bureaucracy moves slowly—especially for the elderly.

The courts delayed hearings. The police dismissed his requests as "a family matter." At one point, a constable even told him, "Baba, samjhauta kar lo. Aapko kaun sambhalega ab?"

For over two months, Shambhu lived off free meals from langars, relied on the generosity of local shopkeepers, and bathed in public facilities. His only company was a small diary in which he scribbled poetry—verses of betrayal, loss, and dignity.

The Turnaround

His story might have been lost forever if not for a young law student named Ayaan, who met Shambhu at a roadside tea stall and, moved by his condition, began documenting his case. Ayaan brought in *HelpAge India*, a well-known NGO, which arranged temporary shelter for Shambhu and connected him to a pro bono legal team.

The legal fight resumed with evidence: property documents, witness testimonies, and proof that Meenakshi had made similar complaints in the past against her own family. Within five months, the **court quashed the protection order** and **restored Shambhu's right to residence**.

But by then, he had already decided—he didn't want to go back.

Dignity Over Walls

Shambhu now lives in an old-age home run by a charitable trust in Sarnath. He spends his days teaching other elderly residents how to read and write Hindi, reciting poetry, and tending to a small garden patch.

When asked if he ever misses his home, he says:

"The walls were mine, but not the people. What's a house if you've been made to feel like a trespasser in your own soul?"

The Unseen Epidemic

Elder abuse is one of India's most underreported social crises. A 2022 HelpAge India report revealed that **1 in 3 elderly parents** face abuse or neglect, mostly from their own children or in-laws. Yet most remain silent—out of fear, shame, or simply having nowhere to go.

When laws intended to protect women are misused to evict elders from their own homes, the **very spirit of justice collapses.**

Shambhu Nath is one among thousands.

But his story—of silence, injustice, and quiet resilience—is now a part of a louder conversation.

A conversation that says: **no one, regardless of age or gender, should ever be abandoned in the name of law.**

Chapter 9

Love, Lies, and Live-In

In modern India, live-in relationships are no longer taboo in metro cities. Courts have recognized them as legitimate under the right to life and personal liberty. But as social norms evolve, so do the complexities—and dangers—within them.

Aman Mehra, a 31-year-old data analyst in Pune, learned this the hard way.

What started as a relationship built on love and companionship turned into a **calculated web of emotional abuse, financial extortion, and legal intimidation**—all within the framework of a live-in arrangement.

The Perfect Match, or So It Seemed

Aman met Nisha (name changed) on a dating app in 2021. She was witty, well-traveled, and worked as a freelance designer. Their connection was instant. After six months of dating, they decided to move in together—a decision Aman made with hope and sincerity.

The first few months were blissful. They shared rent, cooked together, split bills, and even discussed marriage. But over time, subtle red flags began to appear.

Nisha became increasingly controlling—monitoring Aman's phone, questioning his female colleagues, and demanding expensive gifts. When Aman hesitated to spend beyond his means, she accused him of being "stingy" and "emotionally unavailable."

The arguments turned volatile. She once slapped him in a café. Another time, she locked him out of their apartment after a petty disagreement.

Trapped in the Name of Love

Aman didn't speak out. He feared being ridiculed—after all, who would believe a man was being bullied by his girlfriend?

Things escalated when Aman decided to move out. He told Nisha he needed space and suggested ending the relationship amicably.

She didn't take it well.

Within days, Aman received a **legal notice** from Nisha's lawyer, alleging:

> - **Cheating under IPC Section 417**, claiming he had "promised marriage" and backed out.
>
> - **Sexual exploitation** during the live-in period.
>
> - **Mental harassment**, demanding compensation and monthly maintenance.

She also filed a police complaint claiming **outrage of modesty** and demanded an immediate FIR. While the police hesitated, the threat was clear—if Aman didn't pay up, his name would be dragged into a criminal case.

Aman was stunned. "She wasn't a victim. She was vengeful. And the law—meant to protect the vulnerable—was now her weapon."

The Evidence That Saved Him

Fortunately for Aman, he had **documented the relationship**. Screenshots of affectionate messages, shared vacation receipts, and voice recordings of her threats to "ruin his career" became his defense.

He approached a lawyer and filed a counter-complaint, highlighting **extortion and misuse of legal provisions**. When the matter reached court, the judge noted glaring inconsistencies in Nisha's allegations.

She failed to provide any proof of physical abuse or a formal proposal of marriage. The court observed that both parties were consenting adults in a live-in relationship and **dismissed her petition for compensation and maintenance**.

No FIR was lodged.

The Aftermath

Aman had won legally—but emotionally, the scars ran deep. His HR department had initiated an internal inquiry when the complaint surfaced, and though he was cleared, the social whispers continued.

His parents—initially unaware of the live-in—were shattered. The financial toll of legal battles drained his savings.

Today, Aman speaks to college students and working professionals about **legal awareness in relationships**. He urges men to:

> Document interactions.

> Avoid signing financial liabilities under pressure.

> Seek legal consultation early if things go wrong.

The Legal Grey Zone

Indian courts have often ruled that women in live-in relationships are entitled to protection under the **Domestic Violence Act**, and in certain cases, even maintenance. However, there is no **reciprocal protection** for men.

Aman's case reflects the urgent need for:

> Gender-neutral laws for intimate partner violence.

> A legal definition and framework for addressing false cases in live-in dynamics.

> Greater awareness among men about their rights in consensual adult relationships.

When Love Turns Legal

Aman still believes in love. But he believes in caution too.

"Laws should protect the vulnerable—not punish the innocent. A relationship gone wrong shouldn't be a reason to destroy someone's life."

Aman's story is not about blaming women.

It's about **holding individuals accountable**, regardless of gender, and acknowledging that when it comes to relationships, **abuse wears many faces.**

The law must evolve.

Because justice is not just about who shouts louder—it's about who tells the truth.

Chapter 10

The Fight for Fairness

Justice is supposed to be blind—but when laws tilt too heavily in one direction, entire communities are left unprotected. Over the past two decades, India has made enormous strides in legislating against crimes targeting women. Yet, this progress has come with an unintended consequence: the **complete absence of protective laws for male victims**.

But amidst the legal imbalance, a movement is quietly gaining ground—a movement that demands **fairness**, **accountability**, and **gender-neutral justice**. This is the story of that fight.

The Rise of India's Men's Rights Movement

The roots of India's **men's rights movement** can be traced back to the early 2000s, when stories of misuse of **Section 498A of the IPC**—meant to prevent cruelty to women by their husbands and in-laws—began surfacing regularly.

Initially dismissed as isolated cases, the movement gained traction as more men came forward, supported by NGOs and independent lawyers. Today, organizations like the **Save Indian**

Family Foundation (SIFF), **Men Welfare Trust (MWT)**, and **Hridaya** have become the torchbearers for thousands of men who felt abandoned by the legal system.

Their work includes:

➢ Offering legal guidance to falsely accused men.

➢ Running helplines for suicide prevention and mental health support.

➢ Organizing peaceful protests demanding gender-neutral laws.

➢ Filing PILs (Public Interest Litigations) in the High Courts and the Supreme Court.

When Laws Become Weapons

While many laws protecting women are rooted in historical necessity, their misuse has raised questions of fairness. Among the most frequently cited:

➢ **IPC Section 498A** – Dowry harassment: Frequently used to implicate not only husbands but also his entire family.

➢ **The Protection of Women from Domestic Violence Act, 2005** – Offers zero scope for male victims of abuse.

➢ **Sexual Harassment of Women at Workplace (Prevention, Prohibition and Redressal) Act, 2013 (POSH)** – Has no provisions for male employees who face harassment.

➢ **Section 354 IPC** – Assault on a woman with intent to outrage modesty: Can be filed on mere verbal statements without need for corroboration.

These laws, when misused, have destroyed careers, separated fathers from their children, and led to suicides—all without conviction or proof.

A Legal System with One Eye Shut

India's criminal jurisprudence is still largely **gender-biased**. For instance:

> ➢ Men **cannot file** a case of rape or sexual harassment.

> ➢ There is **no legal recognition** of male victims of domestic violence.

> ➢ The burden of proof often falls heavily on the accused man, with immediate arrests and social condemnation.

In a country where laws are rightly made to protect women from systemic violence, the absence of checks and balances has created an **ecosystem ripe for misuse**.

Voices from the Frontlines

Amit Deshpande, founding member of Vaastav Foundation, says:

"We are not against laws that protect women. We are against laws that punish men *without proof*. We want equality, not privilege."

Similarly, **Karan Bedi**, a Supreme Court lawyer who volunteers with SIFF, adds:

"More than 70% of 498A cases don't lead to convictions. But the trauma, the jail time, the social stigma—those are irreversible."

Hope Through Petitions and PILs

Several petitions have been filed in the past decade asking for:

- ➢ **A Commission for Men** (on lines of National Commission for Women)

- ➢ **Gender-neutral laws** on sexual harassment, domestic violence, and child custody

- ➢ **Shared parenting** as a default in custody battles post-divorce

Though most petitions are still pending, public debate around these issues has grown stronger, especially after high-profile suicides of male professionals and young husbands who felt crushed under false cases.

A Changing Social Narrative

Media coverage is slowly beginning to reflect this shift. Stories once relegated to the back pages are now headlining debates.

Mental health experts, too, have chimed in. Many believe that **men's silence around abuse and legal trauma** stems from cultural expectations that view emotional expression in men as weakness.

As a result, depression, substance abuse, and suicide among Indian men—especially those dealing with legal crises—remain dangerously under-addressed.

The Road Ahead

There is still a long way to go. Gender neutrality in Indian law is a sensitive topic, often misrepresented as an anti-woman stance. But those advocating for fairness know the truth:

Fighting for men's rights does not mean denying women theirs. It means building a justice system that protects all.

The real enemy is not feminism, but **misuse**, **bias**, and **silence**.

Conclusion: The Fight is for Balance

This chapter is not just about men's rights.

It's about fairness.

It's about giving every citizen—regardless of gender—a system that listens, investigates, and judges with both eyes open.

It's about replacing the current question—"Who's right?"—with the more important one: **"What's right?"**

Because justice, at its core, is not about protecting one side.

It's about protecting the truth.

Chapter 11

The Other Side of Equality

When we speak of equality in India, the conversation is often limited to empowering women—which, for decades, was essential. But in that focused pursuit, an important truth has been forgotten: **equality is not a one-way street.**

For any society to be truly equal, it must also **protect men from abuse, discrimination, and false victimization**. Ignoring one gender's suffering in the name of empowering another isn't equality—it's imbalance.

This chapter explores the unspoken realities of male vulnerability and the cost of cultural silence around men's pain.

The Social Conditioning of Silence

From the moment they're born, Indian boys are raised with mantras like:

> ➤ *"Mard ko dard nahi hota" (Real men don't feel pain)*

> ➤ *"Ladki hai toh samajh ke rehna padega" (You'll have to adjust for a woman)*

> *"Ghar ka maamla hai, chhupakar niptao" (Keep domestic issues private)*

As a result, when men are subjected to abuse—emotional, physical, or legal—they rarely speak out. Fear of being laughed at, shamed, or not believed keeps them trapped in toxic situations.

Society, law enforcement, and even the judiciary often view men only as **aggressors**, not as **possible victims**.

Media and the Male Narrative

Mainstream media often reinforces the idea of the woman as victim and the man as oppressor. Television shows, films, and even advertising frequently depict men as:

> Drunk, lazy, abusive husbands.

> Emotionally disconnected fathers.

> Predatory coworkers or lovers.

This cultural framing leaves little room for the idea that **a man could be emotionally shattered, physically assaulted, or driven to suicide by harassment.**

Even when male victims do come forward, media coverage is sparse. False cases against men are rarely highlighted with the same urgency or outrage.

Educational Institutions and Bias

Educational programs across schools and colleges emphasize women's safety (rightly so), but they **rarely include modules** on:

- Consent for both genders.

- Recognizing male victims of sexual or emotional abuse.

- Emotional intelligence for boys.

Workshops in schools discuss how boys should not harass girls—but never what to do **if a boy is being harassed or abused**. The result is a generation of young men who are emotionally stunted, unprepared for conflict resolution, and unable to speak up when victimized.

Fathers Without Families

One of the most devastating aspects of gender bias in family courts is seen in **custody battles**. Fathers are often:

- Denied visitation without reason.

- Forced to pay high maintenance even when children are alienated from them.

- Treated as secondary parents, regardless of their emotional involvement or capability.

The law assumes that a child's welfare is best served with the mother, ignoring the importance of a father's role. This bias leaves many men not just without their children, but **without hope**.

Mental Health: The Hidden Epidemic

India has one of the highest suicide rates among men in the world. In 2022, more than **72,000 married men died by suicide**, many citing family issues and legal stress.

Men's mental health remains a **largely invisible crisis**. There are few support systems, therapy is stigmatized, and men are often discouraged from expressing vulnerability.

When society tells men to "man up" instead of "open up," the result is emotional implosion.

False Allegations and Presumed Guilt

In cases of dowry, harassment, or sexual assault, **arrest is often immediate**—especially when the complaint is filed by a woman. Men must then prove their innocence, despite the legal presumption that they're guilty.

This inversion of justice violates the principle of **natural law** and results in:

> ➢ Loss of employment.

> ➢ Social boycotts.

> ➢ Physical assault and defamation.

> ➢ Long-term trauma even after acquittal.

What's worse? The **lack of repercussions** for those who file false cases. No accountability. No deterrence.

Toward a Balanced Society

What does equality really look like?

> ➢ **Gender-neutral laws** that protect all victims.

> ➢ **Sensitivity training** for police and judiciary.

> ➢ **Balanced media narratives** that acknowledge male suffering.

➢ **Educational reform** that teaches boys emotional expression, healthy relationships, and mutual respect.

➢ **Legal consequences for misuse of laws**, just as there are for genuine crimes.

Equality Must Mean Equal Protection

To demand justice for one group by blindfolding it for another is not progressive. True justice acknowledges that **pain doesn't discriminate based on gender.** Neither should laws. Neither should we.

Because for every story of a woman wronged, there are also stories of men destroyed in silence.

The fight for equality must include **the right to be heard, the right to be believed, and the right to be protected**—for every human being.

Chapter 12

The Tragic Case of Atul Subhash

"I am not ending my life. I am donating it to the men's rights movement."

These haunting words were among the final declarations made by **Atul Subhash Bhosale**, a 38-year-old software engineer from Bengaluru, before he died by suicide in December 2024. His death, livestreamed through an 81-minute video confession and followed by a 24-page suicide note, sent shockwaves across India.

Atul's tragedy wasn't just a personal loss—it became a **tipping point** in the growing conversation about **false cases, weaponized legal systems, and the invisibility of male pain** in India's justice narrative.

The Man Behind the Headlines

Atul was not a public figure. He was a middle-class, self-made professional. Friends describe him as kind, calm, deeply spiritual, and conflict-averse. Originally from Maharashtra, he had built a career in Bengaluru's thriving IT sector. He married in 2017—a union that, as he would later recount, began with promises of partnership but ended in **legal warfare, emotional blackmail, and systematic character assassination**.

His relationship deteriorated rapidly, particularly after the birth of his son. According to Atul, what followed was not a bitter divorce, but a **campaign of legal harassment** by his wife and her family.

A Legal Assault on All Fronts

By the time Atul ended his life, he had been battling:

- ➢ **Three different police cases**, including false dowry and domestic violence complaints.

- ➢ **Multiple maintenance and custody petitions** across states.

- ➢ Threats of **false sexual harassment allegations**.

- ➢ Alleged demands for **monetary extortion** running into lakhs.

His suicide note laid it all out in heartbreaking detail. He accused his estranged wife and her parents of **misusing gender-based laws**, leveraging the legal system to financially and socially ruin him.

"I am donating my life to bring light to the misuse of laws. If my death sparks a movement, let it. If it saves another man, it has meaning," Atul wrote.

The Suicide Video: A National Awakening

The 81-minute video Atul recorded just before ending his life was articulate, calm, and shockingly composed. It wasn't a rant—it was a **legal testimony**, a personal eulogy, and a national indictment all rolled into one.

He detailed:

> ➢ Specific FIR numbers.

> ➢ Bank transactions made under duress.

> ➢ Screenshots of WhatsApp chats (later verified).

> ➢ Names of police officials who ignored his pleas.

This wasn't just a cry for help. It was a **call to action**.

Once the video went viral, it triggered a media frenzy. TV debates ignited. Twitter trended #JusticeForAtul and #MenToo. Thousands of men shared their own stories of false cases and legal abuse.

NGOs like **Men Welfare Trust**, **Save Indian Family Foundation**, and **SIFF** held candlelight vigils in multiple cities. Men's rights activists called Atul **"India's Rohith Vemula moment"**—a martyr to a cause hidden in plain sight.

The Police and Judicial Response

While Bengaluru police launched an internal inquiry and promised to review the charges filed against Atul posthumously, **no immediate arrests were made**. His estranged wife denied all allegations, claiming she was being victimized by "patriarchal backlash."

Yet, public sentiment leaned heavily in Atul's favor, as evidence continued to emerge supporting his claims.

Legal scholars debated the ramifications:

> ➤ Why was Atul denied anticipatory bail for over a year?

> ➤ Why did courts not intervene despite evidence of continuous harassment?

> ➤ Why are **false cases so difficult to penalize** under Indian law?

Atul's case became the **centerpiece of a demand for legal reform**.

The Aftermath: A Movement Reignited

In the weeks following his death, activists and citizens came together with specific demands:

> ➤ **A National Commission for Men** to investigate gender-biased laws.

> ➤ **Amendments to IPC Section 498A** to prevent automatic arrest without preliminary inquiry.

> ➤ **Gender-neutral domestic violence laws**.

> ➤ **Penalties for filing false cases**, including perjury and defamation charges.

> ➤ **Mental health helplines for male victims of abuse and legal stress**.

What's perhaps most tragic—and telling—is that these are not radical demands. They are **calls for balance**. For fairness. For human dignity.

A Son's Future, A Father's Legacy

In his final words, Atul expressed sorrow not for his own end, but for his young son. He wrote:

"One day, my child will grow up and Google my name. Let this chapter show him I did not quit. I resisted. I documented. And when no one listened, I gave my life to wake them up."

Today, that son lives with Atul's parents—away from the courtroom battles, but carrying the weight of a legacy too heavy for his young shoulders.

Why Atul's Story Matters

Atul wasn't the first man to end his life under the pressure of false legal cases—and, heartbreakingly, he won't be the last. But his death forced the nation to confront a reality we often ignore:

That **men too can be victims**.

That laws, when misused, don't empower—they destroy.

That justice, when blind to balance, is injustice itself.

Epilogue: The Unfinished Revolution

Atul Subhash Bhosale may be gone, but his story is far from over.

It lives on in petitions to Parliament.

In university debates about gender neutrality.

In every father fighting for custody.

In every man afraid to come forward.

And now, it lives here—in this book, in this chapter, in this sentence.

Because until India's laws protect *all* its citizens, we owe it to Atul—and others like him—to keep telling the truth.

Chapter 13

The Meerut Drum Murder

In March 2025, the people of Meerut woke up to a story that read like the plot of a crime thriller—except it wasn't fiction. It was a real-life tragedy that unfolded in the narrow lanes of Shastri Nagar, and its horror stunned even the most seasoned police officers.

A man's dismembered body was found **stuffed into a plastic drum**, preserved with cement and chemicals, left to decay inside his own home. The man was **Saurabh Rajput**, a 32-year-old former merchant navy officer and entrepreneur. The prime accused? His own wife, **Muskan Rastogi**, and her alleged lover, **Sahil Shukla**.

The case became known nationwide as the **"Meerut Drum Murder"**, and it exposed a brutal, chilling form of domestic crime—one in which **the man was the victim of premeditated murder by his spouse**, a narrative that rarely gets attention in India's crime landscape.

The Victim: Saurabh Rajput

Saurabh Rajput was a man many admired. After years in the merchant navy, he returned to his hometown of Meerut and started a modest printing and packaging business. In 2020, he married Muskan, a well-educated woman from a respectable family. The couple had a young son and lived in a two-story home near the city center.

To outsiders, they seemed happy. But behind closed doors, things had soured. Friends recall Saurabh speaking of emotional distance, growing mistrust, and suspicions of infidelity. He reportedly confronted Muskan multiple times, but chose to "work through it" for the sake of his child.

He didn't know that his wife and her lover were planning his death.

The Murder

On the night of **March 12, 2025**, Muskan allegedly laced Saurabh's food with sedatives. Once unconscious, she called Sahil, and together they **suffocated Saurabh to death using a plastic bag** and a pillow.

But that wasn't enough.

In a cold, calculated attempt to hide the crime, the duo chopped his body into pieces, placed the remains in a large **plastic drum**, poured in **acid and cement**, and sealed it shut. The barrel was left in the storeroom of their house, covered with a cloth.

When neighbors complained of a foul smell days later, Muskan told them it was "a broken sewer line." No one suspected a thing—until a concerned relative, who hadn't heard from Saurabh in over a week, contacted the police.

Discovery and Arrest

Police, upon entering the house, found the barrel. When opened, it revealed a **scene of horror**. Inside was Saurabh's decomposed, chemically-preserved corpse.

Muskan broke down during interrogation and confessed to the crime. Sahil was arrested within hours. Both were charged under **IPC Sections 302 (murder), 201 (destruction of evidence), and 34 (common intent)**.

According to reports, the motive was clear: Muskan wanted to get rid of Saurabh permanently to live with Sahil. She feared a messy divorce, custody battles, and loss of social image. **Murder, they believed, was the easier option.**

The Forgotten Side of Domestic Violence

In India, domestic violence laws and discourse overwhelmingly center around female victims—and rightly so, given centuries of gendered oppression. But the **Meerut Drum Murder** shatters the myth that **only women can be victims within a marriage**.

Here, a man:

> ➢ Was emotionally abused,

> ➢ Cheated on,

> ➢ Murdered by his own wife,

> ➢ And disposed of like garbage.

There were **no early warning systems** for his suffering. No support lines. No legal redressal mechanisms for husbands fearing psychological or physical abuse.

Saurabh had been cornered—with nowhere to turn.

Public and Media Reaction

Initially, the case struggled to gain national traction. A few local newspapers covered it, focusing on the sensational nature of the crime. But men's rights groups called out the **muted outrage** from national media houses.

"If a man had murdered his wife like this, feminists would have held nationwide protests. But now, silence. Why?" — asked a member of the *Men Welfare Trust* on social media.

Eventually, public outrage grew, and the case made it to national primetime. However, what was often missing was a **gendered lens on the male victim**. The discourse remained about "betrayal" or "gruesome murder" but rarely about **domestic abuse of men**, or systemic oversight.

The Legal Battle Ahead

As of the writing of this chapter, Muskan and Sahil remain in judicial custody. The prosecution has demanded a **fast-track trial** given the brutality of the crime.

Saurabh's family, devastated and angry, has started a foundation in his name to raise awareness around male victims of domestic violence and marital manipulation.

His sister said in an interview:

"He was a good man. Quiet. Forgiving. He never raised his voice. Maybe that's why she thought he was weak. But he wasn't weak. He was just decent."

When a Husband is Hunted

The **Meerut Drum Murder** is more than just a crime—it is a revelation. It demands India to finally ask uncomfortable questions:

> ➢ Why don't we recognize male victims of domestic abuse?

> ➢ Why don't Indian laws protect men from violent spouses?

> ➢ Why is male suffering dismissed as rare—or worse, deserved?

Saurabh Rajput's story forces us to confront the other side of marriage—the side where men are trapped, tortured, and, in some cases, eliminated.

His death must not be remembered for its horror alone.

It must be remembered as a **wake-up call**.

Chapter 14

The Snake Bite Deception

In the rural outskirts of Meerut, Uttar Pradesh, death by snake bite isn't unusual. But in April 2025, what appeared to be a tragic accident quickly unraveled into one of the most sinister cases of **premeditated spousal murder** the region had ever seen.

Amit Kashyap, a 25-year-old private school teacher, was found dead in his bedroom—foam around his mouth, a bluish tinge on his skin, and two faint puncture wounds near his neck. His wife, **Ravita**, told neighbors and police that he had died of **snake bites while sleeping**.

The entire village mourned the soft-spoken young man. No one suspected foul play.

Until the postmortem report arrived.

A Death Too Convenient

Doctors found **signs of strangulation**—fractured hyoid bone, deep bruising around the neck, and petechial hemorrhaging in the eyes. The "snake bites" were superficial—**more like pinpricks than venomous punctures**.

There were **no traces of venom** in Amit's blood. No signs of a struggle typical of venom-induced death. Most shockingly, the autopsy noted **ligature marks consistent with manual strangling**, not an animal attack.

Police revisited the scene. No snake was found. No skin sheddings. No trail. No panic from the wife.

Instead, what they uncovered was motive.

The Motive: Lust, Greed, and Escape

Ravita had been **in a long-standing extramarital affair** with a local gym trainer. According to call records and witness testimonies, the relationship had grown serious, and the lovers wanted Amit "out of the picture."

But divorce wasn't an option. Ravita feared losing her share in Amit's ancestral property, and her family worried about the social fallout of a broken marriage in their conservative community.

So she allegedly **plotted his murder**, designed to look like an accident by snakebite—an idea disturbingly inspired by a similar case in Kerala from 2020 where a woman used a cobra to kill her husband.

But unlike the Kerala case, this one lacked planning finesse.

The Web Unravels

Interrogation revealed chilling details.

Ravita confessed that she had initially tried to poison Amit by mixing pesticide in his dinner, but he had vomited it out. Next, she and her lover allegedly visited a quack who suggested **simulating a snakebite** using a syringe or fine needles.

They waited until Amit was asleep and **strangled him slowly with a scarf**, pressing it against his neck until he stopped moving. Then, they used a sharp needle to make two tiny punctures near his neck, hoping it would resemble a snake's bite marks.

The autopsy, however, left no room for doubt.

Both Ravita and her lover were arrested under **IPC Sections 302 (murder), 120B (criminal conspiracy), and 201 (causing disappearance of evidence)**.

When Men Are Targets at Home

Amit's case, while gruesome, highlights a **growing and under-acknowledged pattern in India**—men being murdered by their wives and their lovers. And the murders aren't impulsive—they're **cold, calculated, and often carried out with precision**.

Yet, public discourse continues to cast men solely as perpetrators within domestic spaces. The idea that a woman could be the mastermind behind such a brutal crime still shocks the average citizen, even though the data is slowly showing otherwise.

The Legal and Social Fallout

After the arrests, Amit's family spoke out.

"We thought he had a happy marriage. She used to touch his feet every morning. We never imagined she could be planning his death behind closed doors," said his mother, weeping outside the court.

They demanded that the trial be **fast-tracked**, fearing delays and manipulation of evidence. A local men's rights group took up the case, offering legal aid and pushing for more visibility.

Meanwhile, Ravita's parents claimed that **she was being framed**—a familiar narrative reversal often seen when female accused are presented as victims of circumstance.

But the evidence—call records, messages, and the medical report—left little ambiguity.

The Bigger Picture

Amit's case is not an anomaly. In recent years, India has seen a **rise in cases where husbands have been poisoned, stabbed, or strangled** by their wives—often in collusion with lovers or for property disputes.

Yet, very few of these make headlines. Even fewer are framed as **"crimes against men."**

There are no government campaigns acknowledging male victims of domestic homicide. No national statistics separate these incidents from general murder data. No special provisions exist for men facing psychological or physical abuse from partners.

Why?

Because in the eyes of many, **men are never victims.**

Justice for Amit

The trial in Amit Kashyap's case is ongoing, but the narrative has already shifted. What was once believed to be a tragic death by nature was uncovered as a **planned execution**.

Amit never raised his voice. Never filed a complaint. Never imagined that **his own wife would be his executioner.**

His story is a chilling reminder that **men, too, can be preyed upon in their own homes**, by those they trust the most.

And unless the system acknowledges that, **more lives will be lost in silence, written off as coincidence, or worse—natural causes.**

Chapter 15

The Meerut Triple Murder Case

In the heart of Meerut's crowded **Gudri Bazaar**, where families live stacked floor to ceiling in century-old houses and neighbors know each other's routines better than their own, **three men were murdered in cold blood** on a humid summer night in 2008.

It took the Indian judicial system **16 years** to deliver justice.

In 2024, a district court in Meerut sentenced **10 individuals to life imprisonment** for their role in the brutal triple murder. The victims were:

> **Amit Kumar**, a 26-year-old businessman,

> **Satyendra Pal**, 28, his cousin and assistant,

> **Bhupendra Singh**, 35, their mutual friend.

They were hacked to death in their own home—an attack that was not only premeditated but carried out in front of family members, including women and children. The motive? A combination of **property disputes, ego clashes, and an alleged romantic rivalry**.

But behind the sensational headlines and courtroom drama was a quieter story: that of **men killed not in war or gangland feuds, but by people they trusted.** Their deaths, like so many involving male victims of domestic and neighbourhood disputes, were brushed aside by mainstream media and society.

The Crime Scene

It was the evening of **June 21, 2008**. Amit had returned from his shop, tired but upbeat—he was planning to open a second storefront. As he sat down for dinner, a group of masked men entered the home with iron rods, kitchen knives, and country-made pistols.

There was **no warning, no provocation**. The assailants began attacking the three men indiscriminately. Amit's mother screamed for help, but no one dared to intervene.

By the time the police arrived, **the floor was slick with blood**, the house in shambles. All three men were declared dead on arrival at the local hospital.

Initial suspicion fell on a neighbor's family with whom Amit had had a long-standing dispute over an ancestral lane that both households claimed rights over.

The Investigation: A Test of Endurance

What followed was not a swift path to justice, but a **grueling marathon of hearings, adjournments, missing witnesses, and delays.**

Key hurdles included:

- ➢ Two of the eyewitnesses turned hostile within the first six months.

- ➢ One of the accused fled to Dubai and was only arrested in 2014.

- ➢ Forensic evidence was contested as "inconclusive" due to poor storage.

- ➢ Police officers involved in the initial investigation were transferred multiple times.

The families of the victims, particularly the widowed mothers of Amit and Satyendra, spent over **1,600 days in court**. They mortgaged land, sold jewelry, and lived under threats—just to keep the case alive.

In a deeply patriarchal society, **justice for murdered men is often de-prioritized**, especially when there's no female or child victim involved.

The Verdict: 16 Years Later

In **May 2024**, the district judge finally ruled, sentencing **10 of the 13 accused to life imprisonment**. The remaining three were acquitted due to lack of evidence.

The judgment noted that the murders were "a result of sustained animosity and clear criminal intent," and that "the delay in the justice process should not undermine the seriousness of the crime."

The court also acknowledged that the victims' families had shown "extraordinary perseverance in the face of institutional apathy."

But for the families, the victory was bittersweet.

"We wanted justice—not just for us, but for the men who were brutally silenced and forgotten," said Amit's younger brother, breaking down outside the courthouse. "This isn't closure. This is survival."

Why This Case Matters

In India, when men are victims of violence—especially at the hands of family members, neighbors, or known associates—their deaths are **rarely framed through a lens of gendered vulnerability**. Instead, they're dismissed as "business issues," "masculine clashes," or "personal feuds."

What is missed is the **emotional devastation**, the **erasure of their narrative**, and the **lack of institutional urgency** around such cases.

The Gudri Bazaar triple murder case underscores:

> ➤ **How long justice takes**, especially for male victims.

> ➤ **How little protection men have**, even in legal systems.

> ➤ And how society still fails to recognize that **men can be the ones hunted, not just the ones holding the gun.**

The Lingering Question

If this had been a case of three women or children murdered so brutally, would the headlines have stayed longer? Would the national media have amplified the delays? Would the system have moved faster?

These are not questions to pit genders against one another.

They are questions to remind us that **violence does not discriminate**, and neither should our empathy or our laws.

Chapter 16

Alimony and Adultery
The Chhattisgarh
High Court Ruling

In a landmark judgment that reignited the national conversation around **men's rights in marriage and divorce**, the **Chhattisgarh High Court** in May 2025 ruled that **a wife found guilty of adultery is not entitled to alimony** under Section 125(4) of the Criminal Procedure Code.

The case, while legally significant, was more than a court order—it was a rare moment where **the system validated the emotional and moral trauma faced by a wronged husband**.

The Case: A Marriage in Name Only

The petitioner, **Rajeev Tiwari** (name changed), was a mid-level government employee in Raipur. He had been married to his wife, **Neha**, for 12 years. What began as a typical arranged marriage quickly fell into emotional disconnect and repeated infidelities.

NATIONAL COMMISSION FOR MEN

Over time, Rajeev discovered that Neha was having an affair with **his younger brother**, a man he had helped raise after their father passed away.

It wasn't a passing rumor. Rajeev found WhatsApp messages, hotel receipts, and even eyewitness accounts from neighbors who had seen the two together in compromising situations during his out-of-town postings.

He filed for divorce in 2021 under grounds of **adultery and mental cruelty**—a difficult decision made even harder by the betrayal coming from within his own home.

The Counterattack

Neha, in turn, filed a maintenance petition under **Section 125 CrPC**, seeking **monthly financial support** from Rajeev. She claimed she was unemployed, dependent, and entitled to alimony.

The family court initially ordered **interim maintenance**. Rajeev contested it, presenting clear evidence of her affair. He argued that under **Section 125(4)**—which denies maintenance to a wife who is "living in adultery"—his wife was disqualified.

Neha denied all allegations and alleged "fabrication," but her defense couldn't stand up to the mountain of evidence.

The Judgment: A Legal and Moral Stand

In its verdict, the Chhattisgarh High Court ruled unequivocally in Rajeev's favor. The judgment stated:

"A wife who is proven to be in an adulterous relationship, especially with her husband's close kin, cannot invoke Section

125 to claim maintenance. Doing so would amount to rewarding infidelity and punishing the innocent."

The court further observed that the **duty to maintain a spouse arises from a presumption of moral and legal obligation—** not in situations where that obligation has been violated through deliberate betrayal.

Rajeev was **relieved of all maintenance liabilities**, and the divorce was finalized with **no further financial compensation to the wife**.

The National Ripple Effect

The ruling sparked a wave of discussions across legal and social circles.

Legal experts noted that while adultery was decriminalized by the Supreme Court in 2018 (Joseph Shine v. Union of India), it **remains a valid ground for divorce and disqualification from alimony** under civil law.

What made this case stand out was:

➤ The **boldness** of the judgment in a judiciary often seen as conservative in divorce matters.

➤ The **public acknowledgment** of the husband's emotional trauma.

➤ The reaffirmation that **marriage is a two-way contract**, not an unconditional support obligation.

Men's rights organizations hailed it as a **"moment of rare judicial empathy"**, while many women's rights activists argued that it should not set a precedent for denying genuine claimants.

Rajeev's Words: A Voice Rarely Heard

In a rare interview, Rajeev shared:

"I didn't want revenge. I just wanted dignity. I had lived for years knowing my wife was cheating with my own blood—and still I supported her. But when she demanded alimony, that was my breaking point. Why should betrayal be rewarded with a monthly cheque?"

He recounted the psychological toll—the shame, the isolation, the mockery from neighbors, and the pain of family fallout. But he said the judgment gave him **back his self-worth**.

When Courts See the Whole Picture

The Indian legal system often operates in binaries—men as providers, women as dependents. But real life is messier. And Rajeev's case proved that **law must account for betrayal, manipulation, and abuse—regardless of gender.**

It also highlighted a harsh truth: **many Indian men stay silent in the face of infidelity, fearing social stigma, legal complexity, and emotional blackmail.**

The Chhattisgarh ruling gave such men a rare beacon of hope— a signal that their pain, too, deserves redress.

The Road Ahead

This case has spurred legal debates on broader reforms:

> ➤ Should **marital misconduct impact financial settlements** more rigorously?

> ➤ Can there be **mandatory pre-litigation mediation** in maintenance disputes?

> ➤ Do we need a **gender-neutral maintenance law** that accounts for both partners' earning potential and conduct?

Most importantly, it has prompted a deeper cultural conversation on **morality, accountability, and equality in relationships**.

Justice, Not Just Gender

Rajeev's case is not about punishing women.

It's about **not punishing men for being betrayed**.

It's about making alimony a tool of support—not an instrument of exploitation.

It's about restoring the idea that dignity and loyalty matter—even in the courtroom.

Chapter 17

Supreme Court's Stance on Alimony Demands

"A divorced wife is entitled to a life of dignity, not to parity with her ex-husband's wealth."

With these words, the **Supreme Court of India**, in a December 2024 verdict, drew a firm line between **financial security** and **entitlement**.

This case—and its historic judgment—didn't just redefine the scope of alimony. It sparked a critical national debate on the **limits of matrimonial maintenance**, especially in an era where traditional roles are rapidly evolving, and women are increasingly independent.

But most significantly, the verdict gave a long-ignored voice to **men caught in exploitative post-divorce financial arrangements**—many of whom were forced to continue paying lifelong maintenance even in cases of short marriages or mutual breakups.

The Case in Question

The petitioner, **Arvind Sharma** (name changed), a senior IT consultant in Gurugram, had been divorced for four years. His marriage had lasted barely 18 months. The separation was mutual—but shortly afterward, his ex-wife filed a petition for enhanced alimony.

She claimed that Arvind's annual salary had increased significantly post-divorce and argued that **her standard of living should match his current income**, despite the fact that she had **no children to support**, and had since moved in with her parents.

She demanded:

> ➢ A monthly alimony of ₹1.25 lakh.

> ➢ 50% share in Arvind's property purchased post-divorce.

> ➢ One-time compensation for "emotional trauma."

The family court initially ruled in her favor—stating that Arvind's "improved financial status" should translate to "enhanced post-divorce support."

Arvind challenged the order in the **Supreme Court**.

The Judgment: Equity Over Equality of Outcome

The bench, comprising Justices Ajay Rastogi and Bela Trivedi, overturned the lower court's ruling. In a strongly worded verdict, the court said:

"Maintenance under Section 125 CrPC is meant to prevent destitution—not to provide a lifestyle upgrade based on the rising fortunes of a former spouse."

It held that:

> The obligation to pay maintenance must be rooted in **need**, not in comparative wealth.

> Alimony is not a tool to ensure **lifestyle parity** after the end of the marital relationship.

> **Marriage is not a lifelong annuity**—especially in the absence of children or demonstrated dependency.

The court further stated that **a divorced woman is free to pursue her own career, education, or income**, and cannot rely indefinitely on an ex-husband who has moved on.

Impact on the Ground

The judgment was a **watershed moment** for many divorced men in India. Men's rights groups hailed the verdict as **"progressive, rational, and constitutionally sound."**

In multiple states, lawyers began citing the ruling in ongoing cases, using it as precedent to challenge excessive alimony awards.

But it wasn't just about money—it was about **fairness**.

For years, men like Arvind had silently complied with maintenance orders that, in some cases, left them financially crippled. Many couldn't remarry, buy a home, or plan a future—because **a failed marriage had turned into a lifelong financial liability**.

This ruling gave them a fighting chance to reclaim their independence.

Criticism and Counterviews

Women's rights advocates expressed concern that the verdict could be misused to **evade genuine responsibilities**, especially in rural areas where women are still financially vulnerable.

But the court addressed this directly, noting:

"The ruling does not exempt husbands from maintenance. It merely **clarifies that such support must be reasonable, time-bound, and proportional** to the needs and conduct of both parties."

It emphasized that women with no education, no job prospects, or children to raise would still be entitled to rightful support. But **misuse of maintenance as post-divorce leverage must stop**.

A Cultural Shift in Motion

This judgment signals a **larger societal transformation**:

> ➤ More Indian women are choosing careers and financial independence.

> ➤ Men are beginning to speak out about legal and emotional exploitation.

> ➤ Courts are slowly moving away from **one-size-fits-all alimony rulings**.

Importantly, it brings into focus the **emotional trauma of men post-divorce**—something often ignored.

Men like Arvind described living in "legal limbo" for years—unable to move on, afraid of financial instability, and constantly judged by courts that presumed guilt in silence.

Redefining Modern Alimony

In essence, the Supreme Court reminded the nation that **alimony is not a punishment**. It's a protection—for those who need it. Not a reward for failed relationships. Not an economic settlement for emotional grievances.

The judgment opens the door for:

> - **Capped durations of maintenance** based on marriage length.

> - Consideration of the woman's earning potential and conduct.

> - Use of **mediation panels** to resolve maintenance issues outside courts.

Closing Thoughts: Equality in Exit

Marriages may not always work—but the law's role is not to extend punishment after the relationship ends.

By reinforcing the principle that **support must stem from necessity, not nostalgia or revenge**, the court has taken a bold step toward true gender fairness.

And for thousands of Indian men battling excessive alimony demands, this ruling isn't just relief—

It's **recognition**.

Chapter 18

The Ravi Mohan Divorce Saga

In the glossy world of cinema, marriages sparkle under studio lights, but off-screen, even stars crumble under the weight of toxic relationships. In early 2025, Tamil actor **Ravi Mohan**—a beloved icon in South Indian cinema—became the face of **celebrity divorce wars**, when his 18-year-long marriage to his wife **Aarti** unraveled under public scrutiny.

What made this case explosive wasn't just the emotional drama—it was the **demand for ₹40 lakh per month in alimony**, a sum so staggering it stunned even the legal community.

The Ravi Mohan divorce wasn't just a media circus. It exposed how **men, even those successful and respected, can be emotionally, financially, and socially cornered** in family courts.

The Man Behind the Spotlight

Ravi Mohan, known for his disciplined lifestyle, clean public image, and consistently hit films, had always kept his personal life private. He met Aarti during his early acting days—she came from a business family and stood by him during his initial years of struggle.

They married in 2006. Over the years, their marriage appeared stable, and Aarti was often seen at award ceremonies and public events. They had two children and lived in a luxury residence in Chennai.

But in early 2025, the façade shattered.

The Filing: Accusations and Asks

Aarti filed for divorce citing **"emotional neglect, incompatibility, and breach of marital responsibilities."** But what grabbed headlines was her financial claim:

"I have maintained a public image, raised children alone, and stood in the shadow of his success. I deserve ₹40 lakh a month to maintain the lifestyle I was accustomed to," she said in her petition.

She also sought:

> ➢ Primary custody of both children.

> ➢ A 50% share in Ravi's real estate, including homes bought before their marriage.

> ➢ Compensation for "emotional distress and loss of identity."

The media lapped it up. TV debates sparked discussions on whether women "deserve half" of their ex-husband's wealth. Social media was torn between support for Aarti and sympathy for Ravi.

Ravi's Response: A Rarity in Masculine Silence

Unlike most male celebrities who shy away from personal controversies, Ravi issued a **dignified but firm statement**:

"While I respect the sanctity of marriage and appreciate the years we shared, I cannot allow false narratives and disproportionate demands to tarnish my reputation or impact the future of my children."

Ravi's legal team contested the alimony demand, stating that:

> ➤ Aarti had investments, rental income, and luxury assets of her own.

> ➤ She had access to personal staff, vehicles, and property post-separation.

> ➤ She had no financial dependency on him, and the demand was **"an attempt to secure a post-divorce fortune, not maintain subsistence."**

The Gendered Backlash

Despite presenting clear financial records, Ravi was **villainized in some sections of the press**. News tickers screamed, "Superstar Abandons Wife?" while others speculated about affairs and hidden assets.

Men's rights advocates called out the **hypocrisy**:

"If a female actor were asked to pay ₹40 lakh a month to her ex-husband, there would be nationwide outrage. But when a man pushes back against excessive alimony, he's labeled heartless," said a spokesperson from Men Welfare Trust.

NATIONAL COMMISSION FOR MEN

The Legal Fight: High Stakes, Higher Costs

Ravi and Aarti's case is now being heard in a family court in Chennai, with **one of the most high-profile legal teams in the South**. Custody remains a fiercely contested issue. Ravi is seeking shared parenting, while Aarti wants sole custody.

The court has appointed a **child psychologist** to assess the children's well-being—a progressive step rarely seen in celebrity divorces.

As for alimony, the court has asked both parties to submit detailed affidavits of income, assets, and liabilities. While the ₹40 lakh claim has not yet been granted, **interim maintenance of ₹5 lakh per month** was allowed pending final decision.

The Bigger Picture: When Divorce Becomes a Jackpot

What Ravi's case reveals is a **troubling trend in high-profile divorces**:

> ➢ Exaggerated maintenance claims disconnected from actual dependency.

> ➢ Use of children as leverage in custody battles.

> ➢ Societal bias that sees successful men as bottomless financial reservoirs.

In many such cases, the law becomes **less about justice and more about negotiation of wealth**, with men expected to "pay up for peace."

Celebrity or Not, Men Bleed Too

Ravi Mohan's case isn't just about crores and custody. It's about **how even the most powerful men can be made vulnerable by a legal system that assumes financial responsibility without equitable emotional accountability.**

He once said in a private interview:

"People think I'm fighting because of money. I'm fighting because I want fairness. I want to be a father, not just an ATM."

Conclusion: From Star Hero to Symbol of Resistance

As his legal battle continues, Ravi has become a **quiet symbol for countless divorced Indian men**—men who aren't superstars, but who carry the same scars. Men fighting to stay in their children's lives. Men who want closure, not compensation. Men who loved, lost, and are now told to pay for it forever.

The Ravi Mohan divorce saga isn't just gossip.

It's a glimpse into the price men often pay—in private—when public systems fail to protect them.

Chapter 19

The Road Ahead Advocating for Men's Rights

For centuries, Indian society has celebrated the resilience of women against patriarchal oppression—and rightly so. Laws, policies, and public movements have arisen to protect and empower women. But somewhere along the way, **we stopped asking a fundamental question**:

Can men be victims too?

As the previous chapters in this book have shown—through case after painful case—the answer is not only yes, but **urgently, unambiguously yes**.

And yet, the system doesn't reflect that reality.

In India today, while women are protected under multiple gender-specific laws, **there is no comprehensive legal framework recognizing men as victims** of domestic violence, false accusations, financial exploitation, or emotional abuse.

There is no national helpline. No ministry for men. No male-centric legal aid policy.

The road ahead for men's rights in India is not just about countering false cases. It's about creating **an equal, compassionate, and just system—for all genders.**

The Legal Reforms We Need

1. Gender-Neutral Laws

Domestic violence, sexual harassment, and abuse laws must be made gender-neutral, recognizing that **abuse is about power, not gender.** Sections like IPC 498A, which criminalizes cruelty by husbands and their families, should have equivalent safeguards for male victims of spousal abuse.

2. False Case Penalties

There must be **strict, time-bound punishment** for proven false accusations. False rape and dowry allegations not only destroy lives—they also dilute the credibility of genuine cases.

3. Shared Parenting in Custody Laws

Child custody should not be a reward for the mother or a punishment for the father. Laws must be amended to presume **equal parental access** unless proven otherwise.

4. Time-Capped Alimony

Alimony and maintenance must be based on **need, duration of marriage, and mutual contribution**—not lifelong payments that trap men in financial slavery.

5. Men's Commission

A **National Commission for Men**, modeled after NCW, should be established to look into male-specific issues, data, and legal challenges.

A Mental Health Crisis Unspoken

Many male victims never make it to court. **They die in silence—often by suicide.**

According to NCRB data, over **70% of suicides in India are male**, with family problems, unemployment, and marital stress among the top causes.

Men are rarely taught to express pain. Society calls them weak if they cry. Courts view them suspiciously if they claim victimhood. Police mock them when they report abuse.

The result? **An epidemic of emotional isolation.**

We need:

> ➢ **Men's support groups** and helplines in every state.

> ➢ **School curriculums that redefine masculinity**—not as stoicism, but as emotional openness.

> ➢ Mandatory **gender-sensitization training for police and judges**—not just to protect women, but to protect fairness.

Rising Voices, Emerging Movements

In recent years, grassroots groups like **Save Indian Family Foundation (SIFF)**, **Men Welfare Trust**, and **Confidare** have provided legal aid, counseling, and community support for male victims. Their work is often dismissed as "anti-women," but in truth, these organizations advocate not against women—but **for justice**.

They run:

> ➤ Weekly support meetings for suicidal men.

> ➤ Legal bootcamps for fighting false cases.

> ➤ National awareness campaigns like **Men's Day Marches** and **Black Ribbon Movements**.

Yet, they lack institutional funding, political backing, or mainstream media support.

The Media's Role: A Double-Edged Sword

Media narratives continue to **frame men primarily as perpetrators**, even when proven otherwise. False rape accusations make front-page news; acquittals, if they come years later, are buried in corner columns.

TV soaps, movies, and news anchors often **mock male pain**—portraying abused husbands as cowards or jokes. This cultural bias seeps into policy, judiciary, and police response.

We must demand:

> ➤ **Balanced journalism** that follows cases beyond initial accusation.

> ➤ **Fair reporting** on male victimhood and due process.

> ➤ Representation of men's issues in entertainment media—not as villains, but as humans.

The Real Feminism Includes Men Too

This book is not anti-women.

It is **pro-equality.**

Real feminism fights for fairness for all. It does not ignore the suffering of one group to champion another. It does not pit genders against each other but **seeks to free all from the shackles of rigid expectations**.

Just as women deserve safety, dignity, and justice—**so do men**.

A Call to Conscience

As a nation, we are evolving. But evolution must be inclusive.

If we believe in justice, we must believe that **truth has no gender**. Pain has no gender. And rights must have no gender.

The road ahead will not be easy. It requires courage—to admit imbalance, to question old beliefs, to stand up for the silenced.

Let us begin.

Not just for the men whose stories were told in this book—but for the millions whose stories are yet to be heard.

Silent scars may not bleed, but they still ache.

And it's time the nation listens.

The Final Chapter

This may be the final chapter of *Silent Scars*, but if we continue to ignore the silent suffering of men, then a future book on this subject might one day include someone you know—your brother, your friend, your son, your colleague, or perhaps even you. If the largest democracy in the world still does not see the need for a **National Commission for Men**, then we are complicit in the pain yet to unfold. Let me be clear—when I say we need a Commission for Men, I do **not** mean we don't need one for women. We absolutely do. Women have endured generations of injustice, and the fight for their rights must continue with full force. But now, it's time to extend that conversation. **It's time to save our men, too.** Not by taking away from anyone else—but by standing for **everyone** who bleeds, breaks, and bears their scars in silence.

Appendices

Appendix A: Support Helplines for Men in India

These helplines offer emotional, legal, and practical support to male victims of abuse, false cases, or distress.

Men's Rights Helpline (SIFF)
Description: Operated by Save Indian Family Foundation for men facing false 498A/DV cases
Contact: +91-8882-498498

Men Welfare Trust (MWT)
Description: Emotional and legal aid for men in distress
Contact: www.menwelfare.in

Confidare Men's Rights Community
Description: Legal help and peer support across major cities
Contact: support@confidareindia.com

Vaastav Foundation
Description: Counselling and guidance for men facing matrimonial harassment
Contact: +91-9582-498498

Save Family Foundation
Description: PAN-India helpline for victims of false cases
Contact: +91-8826-498498

SIF One Weekly Meetups
Description: Every Sunday in major cities for emotional/legal support
Contact: www.saveindianfamily.org

Appendix B: Legal Resources and NGO Contacts

Legal Provisions Commonly Used Against Men:
- IPC 498A – Cruelty by husband or relatives
- Section 125 CrPC – Maintenance for wife
- The Domestic Violence Act, 2005 – Does not include men as complainants
- Section 354 IPC – Outraging modesty of a woman
- Section 376 IPC – Rape (non-gender neutral)

Important Judgments:
- Rajesh Sharma v. State of UP (2017)
- Joseph Shine v. Union of India (2018)
- Supreme Court, Dec 2024 – Maintenance not to be parity-based post-divorce

NGOs Actively Working on Men's Issues:

Save Indian Family Foundation (SIFF) - Bengaluru/Delhi - www.saveindianfamily.org

Men Welfare Trust - Delhi - www.menwelfare.in

Confidare - Bengaluru - www.confidareindia.com

Vaastav Foundation - Mumbai - www.vaastav.org

Indian Family Foundation - Pune - www.indianfamilyfoundation.in

Appendix C: Sample Legal Formats for False Case Defense

1. Application for Anticipatory Bail under Section 438 CrPC

IN THE COURT OF SESSIONS JUDGE, _____

Anticipatory Bail Application

Applicant: [Full Name]
S/o: [Father's Name]
R/o: [Address]
Versus
State of [State Name]

Respected Sir/Madam,

The applicant respectfully submits:

1. That he apprehends arrest in FIR No. ___ dated ___ registered at PS ___ under Sections 498A/406/34 IPC.
2. That the FIR is false, fabricated, and maliciously filed by the complainant (wife) with an intent to harass.
3. That the applicant is ready to cooperate with the investigation.

PRAYER:
In view of the above, the applicant may be granted anticipatory bail.

Place: _____
Date: _____
(Signature)

2. Complaint to SP/DCP for Misuse of IPC 498A

To,
The Superintendent of Police,
[District Name]

Subject: Request for inquiry into false complaint under IPC 498A

Respected Sir/Madam,

I, [Full Name], wish to bring to your kind attention that my wife [Name] has filed a false complaint against me and my family under Section 498A IPC, FIR No. _ dated _ at [Police Station].

This appears to be done with an ulterior motive of extortion and personal vendetta. I request your office to conduct a fair and impartial investigation before any coercive action is taken.

Sincerely,
[Your Name & Contact Details]

3. Application for Shared Parenting / Visitation Rights

IN THE FAMILY COURT OF _____

Petitioner: [Full Name]
Versus
Respondent: [Spouse's Name]

Subject: Petition for shared parenting and visitation rights under Guardians and Wards Act, 1890

The petitioner respectfully submits:

- That the marriage between petitioner and respondent is under dissolution.
- That the petitioner has been denied access to his minor child [Name, Age] without any just cause.
- That shared parenting is in the best interest of the child.

Prayer:
Allow the petitioner visitation and shared custody of the minor child as per law.

Date: _____
(Signature)

About the Author

Dr. Nitya Prakash is an award-winning author, education reformist, and international speaker whose work spans the intersection of learning, law, and social justice. With over a decade of leadership in the global education and innovation sector, he has been at the forefront of transforming lives through knowledge, empathy, and advocacy.

Nominated for the Nobel Peace Prize in 2022 and recognized among India's Top 15 Inspiring Entrepreneurs in 2025, Dr. Prakash is the CEO of Quality New Zealand Education, an institution bridging opportunities between India and New Zealand for talent development and global mobility. His work has been endorsed by iconic personalities including Sir Richard Hadlee, Stephen Fleming, Daniel Vettori and Brendon McCullum.

He is also a published author of 14 bestselling books, including the critically acclaimed Education 2050. The Hindustan Times described him as an "author at his best," applauding his ability to capture the pulse of real social issues with deep human sensitivity.

National Commission for Men: Silent Scars stems not only from his extensive research but also from lived experience—both personal and witnessed. Through this book, Dr. Prakash lends voice to countless unheard men across India who have been denied justice, misunderstood, or overlooked by the system.

Far from being anti-women, his work calls for inclusive justice—where equity is not gendered, and compassion is not selective. He is a firm believer in the power of dialogue, reform, and balance in shaping a better tomorrow for both men and women.

When not writing or leading strategic education initiatives, Dr. Prakash serves as a mentor with NITI Aayog's Atal Innovation Mission and collaborates with premier Indian institutions like IIT Bombay and Chandigarh University.

He believes stories can heal—and that justice must begin where silence ends.

He can be reached at

prakashnitya@ymail.com | www.nityaprakash.in

www.ingramcontent.com/pod-product-compliance
Lightning Source LLC
Chambersburg PA
CBHW032101020426
42335CB00011B/436